Too Many Irons in the Fire
…and They're All Smoking

Other books by Cynthia Bond Hopson

Bad Hair Days, Rainy Days, and Mondays
Times of Challenge and Controversy
Wiggle Tales

Too Many Irons in the Fire

in the Fire

...and They're All Smoking

Cynthia Bond Hopson

DIMENSIONS
FOR LIVING
NASHVILLE

TOO MANY IRONS IN THE FIRE
...AND THEY'RE ALL SMOKING

Copyright © 2008 by Dimensions for Living

This book is printed on acid-free paper.

Library of Congress Cataloging-in-Publication Data

Hopson, Cynthia A. Bond, 1955-
   Too many irons in the fire : and they're all smoking / by Cynthia Bond Hopson.
      p. cm.
   ISBN 978-0-687-49167-4 (binding: adhesive-perfect : alk. paper)
1. Christian women—Prayers and devotions.   I. Title.
   BV4844.H655 2008
   242′.643—dc22

                                                    2008008646

08 09 10 11 12 13 14 15 16 17—10 9 8 7 6 5 4 3 2 1

MANUFACTURED IN THE UNITED STATES OF AMERICA

Contents

On the highway of life, the longer you're on the highway,
the faster the speed limit seems to be.
—Frank and Ernest *comic strip*

A Word from the Author

My sisters, my friends, I wish I knew where the phrase "too many irons in the fire" came from, but every time I hear those six words an image immediately pops into my head. I see myself juggling twenty-five balls. One is in the air and the other twenty-four are all over the floor—I have unsuccessfully tried to do too many things at once. Someone somewhere called it *multitasking,* and women bought the concept like a cone of homemade rocky road ice cream on a hot summer afternoon. We believed if we couldn't do a million things simultaneously, something must be wrong with us. You can call it multitasking if you like; I call it sheer stupidity. As Forrest Gump, one of my favorite movie characters, might say, "Stupid is as stupid does." I'm not calling you stupid—I am strictly talking about Cynthia Ann.

When I look at the past month, stupidity is the only thing you could call it. With a capital *S*. I said I'd write a chapter for another book but didn't ask when the deadline was. When it turned out to be February 28, I should've said right then and there I couldn't do it because of all the other stuff that already had to be done. Did I do that? No. Instead, I took on two more speaking engagements (about self-care and time management, of all things!) to go with what was already on the calendar. Then I learned that my husband and I were going to move, and we went house hunting. Then I had the nerve to act shocked when I missed my February deadline. Now today, after too many meetings about too many meetings and other stuff I still don't understand, I am trying to write a book called *Too Many Irons in the Fire . . . and They're All Smoking!* Like I said—sheer stupidity. Plain and simple.

I found myself thinking, "If I can just get to the end of the month, I'm going to take some time off." I now understand that if I'm not careful, when the end of the month comes I'll be making some of the same stupid scheduling blunders again. My husband, Roger, calls it my "be all things to all people" syndrome. Being all things to all people—another phrase that conjures up images. You want to be it all, do it all, have it all, and know it all. Forget about it. You can't. That's what you've got God for, and since God created time, place, and space, that job's already taken. You'll have to find another way to make the world better; God will take care of us and all that concerns us.

Start today. Make a fire if you must, but be sure to take a seat and bask in the beautiful glow. Warm and renew yourself by the embers of yesterday, and vow to do something different today. Just because you made poor choices then doesn't mean you have to make them now. God is waiting to bless you with wisdom, abundance, and peace—hold still and be blessed.

Dedication and Thanks

I thank God for my life, for a faith that sustains me, and for family and friends who bless my heart and lift my spirit. Alex Haley is often credited with saying, "Any time you see a turtle on top of a fence, you know he had some help." I'm no turtle, but I had tons of help getting to this place, and I am grateful for the notes of encouragement, the wise words, and the opportunity to make a difference. I won't try to count my blessings and name them one by one, but I am grateful to God for every good and perfect thing (and the bad and the imperfect too, now that I think about it).

This book is for everyone who helped make this project possible:

For Roger, my hero and the wind beneath my wings,
without whose help there would be a whole lot less
wisdom and encouragement

and
our wonderful and delightful children, Marcos and Angela,
who inspire me with their unconditional love and support

and
the world's cutest and smartest grandchildren
(and their beautiful mom, Regina)
Kiera, Terrell, Maya, and Morgan

For Alvis Marie, Emma, Bernice, Lula, Mildred,
Sallie, and Ann,
women who inspire me with their sheer will, true grit,
and amazing fortitude

For my phenomenal sisters, especially Sophia,

and in memory of
John A. Bond Jr., Carey Bowles, Alvin and Orelia,
Shady and Carmella, Clara and John Amos,
Isaiah and Irene, A.G.,
and especially Mama and Miss Becky

For all who have been or will be blessed and inspired by
the gifts God gives me to share.

To God be the glory.

If life gives you lemons, squeeze the li'l suckers
and let 'em know who's boss.
—Author

1. If You're Going Through Hell, Keep On Going.

Scripture: Jeremiah 29:10-14; Job 1:1–2:10

Something about adversity must prompt people to say things that get repeated often enough to become clichés. Things like "Your attitude determines your altitude," "When life gives you lemons, make lemonade," "You can choose to get bitter or better"—the list goes on. I've even helped move some of them to superstar status. But as I thought about life's lemons and "showing the li'l suckers who's boss," images of my mother whipping my butt popped up.

I grew up in an era where spankings were not just expected, they were given often and heartily (seemingly with glee, but for my own good, of course). The spankings made me cry, but my mother kept whipping to make me stop crying. If I didn't cry, she'd go into the "Oh, so you're not gonna cry?" mode and whip some more, because crying must've signaled submission and not crying signaled defiance—I don't know. I finally concluded that I was going to get punished, but I could decide how I took it—with dignity, standing tall and crying just enough, or kicking and scrambling to avoid the licks.

Life is like that too. There's going to be rain—nobody knows how much or how often, but expect it. Heartache and pain and things we can't pronounce are real—you name it and there's a picture of somebody we know beside it in the dictionary. We can be taken under if we're not firmly grounded in our faith, and then it's still tough. Sometimes gathering the strength and fortitude to stand takes more courage than actually waging the battle, so we must first decide if we're going to live to fight another day or if we're going to waste energy on distractions.

And distractions are an energy buster—look at Job. Satan knew that Job's heart belonged to God and nothing would change that, but he figured if he hit Job in the gut—if he took his stuff and his family—that would break him. Here's the beautiful part of the story—the more Satan attacked him, the more Job depended on God. He knew the storm was a test, and not only had he studied for the test, he knew that with God's help he'd pass it with flying colors. Like I often say, God wanted to give Job something to shout about.

Talking about tests and testimonies brings Mrs. Callie Sue Graves Brown immediately to mind. When I was growing up, she and her husband of sixty-six years, Mr.

Buster, were our neighbors and were like an extra set of parents. They still are. Whenever and wherever you see Miss Callie Sue, she has a word from God for you. I believe she knows the whole Bible, because she doesn't just quote the Scriptures, she lives them. One day I got a call that the two of them had been in a terrible automobile accident, and I went to the hospital to see Miss Callie Sue. She had taken the brunt of the injuries, her body was battered and broken, and she could hardly see, but she was praising the Lord that things were as well as they were. Her words that day inspire me still: "If I praise him when I'm up, you know I'm going to praise him when I'm down."

Yes, ma'am, I know and I'm telling you that whether we are up or down, God will be there, helping us, carrying us, pushing us, loving us, and that's a darn fine reason to shout today. The moral of this lesson is don't give up; help is on the way. It sounds terribly trite, but know that God loves you. A song by Rodney Atkins offers words of encouragement: "If you're going through hell, keep on going. . . . You might get out before the devil even knows you're there."

That's what I'm counting on—living triumphantly.

Thank you, Lord, for keeping me close and helping me weather the storms. Whether it's rainy or sunny or somewhere in between, I will praise you. Amen.

Lord have mercy, how's she even get them britches on?
—Trace Adkins

2. I'm Not Fat, I'm Filled Out.

Scripture: Song of Solomon 4:1-7

I've stopped letting people hurt my feelings about my weight. I am not fat, I am filled out, and there is a difference. About three inches worth. Granted, if I stay on this path I may get fat someday, but right now I'm just stout. Every time I say "stout" I think about visiting my best friend, Lois. Her mother, Miss Odessa, would always greet me warmly with, "Baby, I believe you've stoutened up." We'd laugh at her familiar opening, but I didn't mind.

With that said, some of the people in my business now don't know me well enough to be discussing my size. With Miss Odessa, we went back to before the Kennedy and Martin Luther King assassinations and the Vietnam War. Now when someone says, "Girl, you sure have gotten big," I look them in the eye and reply, "That really hurt my feelings because I worked hard to look nice today." That usually shuts them down. Then they add, "But you look good," which is where they should've started.

My friend Nick swears it doesn't matter if he's won the Nobel Prize in Literature (his goal) or cured cancer (not in his job description); the first thing small-minded people want to talk about is his weight. It took me a while to get the courage to challenge them when they talk about mine, but I realized if I didn't deal with their insensitivity, I would forever be on the defensive. My weight is just that—mine. While that size fourteen with the elastic has started to be a challenge, I am more than a discussion about my gut, butt, and school-marm arms (you know, the loosey-goosey part above your elbow that jiggles when you wave hello).

Seriously, though, weight-related issues are causing insurance rates to skyrocket and dividing government entities that don't know how to help or stem the problem. Obesity and eating disorders are dominating the news, and rightfully so, because many of us didn't stop with "filled out"—we got off at the next station, "'bout to be fat," and had such a good time we went to the next level, "Gotta wear ugly clothes designed by wacky people who run overpriced stores." There must be a law that says if you're bigger than a size twelve, report to the sporting goods section to buy a tent, because finding something cute in plus sizes is work. And be clear, if you wear bigger sizes, you can't just buy any brand and any style; you have to buy the ones designed with you in mind–vertical stripes, elastic sides, and enough material so you don't get hurt trying to get in them.

Some of our children are about to be the size of the biblical giant Goliath. The other extreme is movie stars, teenagers, and others who literally starve themselves to death because their self-image is unhealthy. There has to be a happy medium. I eat because I enjoy food, but I know that I can't keep going up without my health declining.

If I want to be mobile, and I do, I must make some changes. Heavy breathing is all right if there's something fun going on, but not when you're trying to get up the steps. I know that the heavier I get, the more risk I run for developing certain kinds of cancers and other dreadful but preventable diseases. Since I'd rather spend my money shopping instead of on prescription drugs, I say let's take preventative measures and really feel good and look even better.

Lord, you've created so many wonderful things. Help us enjoy them in moderation and be reminded always that our bodies are your temple. Amen.

Nobody can do for little children what a grandparent can do.
—Alex Haley

3. Grandbabies Are Grand in Every Way.

Scripture: 2 Timothy 1:3-7

When Terrell and Kiera came to the daycare door that warm April day, and Terrell threw himself in my arms with a "There's my grandma" pronouncement, I melted and I've never been the same. When Maya came last election day after an almost ten-year lull, she bowled all of us over and now runs every Hopson household between Memphis and Lebanon, Tennessee. Our newest granddaughter, Morgan, has done the same things.

Morgan and Maya are too young, but Terrell and Kiera are old enough now that I can take them to the movie, go on special dates with them, teach them to cook, impart grandmotherly wisdom, and have a good excuse to go to the children's museum and Chuck E. Cheese Pizza Parlor. I don't know who has more fun, them or me, but they indulge me. They also love Rice Crispy Treats (OK, so they give me an excuse to make them for myself too, just in case they come by), and when I know they're coming, we're clear about what has to happen.

I hadn't given much thought to being a grandparent. I knew I wanted to be a good one, because I believe children who have known their grandparents are richer because of it. When I think about one of my favorite children's sermons, I smile. The sermon was one of those question-and-answer sessions that most experienced preachers avoid, because once you ask questions you never know where you'll have to go. The minister asked the children, "What do you want to be when you grow up?" The smallest boy yelled, "A granddaddy!"

I know how he felt, because I had some of the finest grandparents anywhere and I love being a grandparent. It gives you bragging rights. I was doing a radio interview the other morning, and the host told me during the break that he would ask about my children and grandchildren. I warned him that they were really cute and smart and once I got started with the "grandbaby chronicles" it would be difficult to focus. He said if he asked about mine, then he could talk about his. We had a ball.

I told my daughter-in-law that I had to have pictures— lots of them. For Mother's Day this year she got me one of those accordion-type albums chock-full of pictures, so at the first mention of grandchildren, I'm ready. That's what grandparents are supposed to do—have pictures and spoil grandchildren. It ain't necessarily so for some of us, though. If you've been drafted back into child raising service, that's totally different from spoiling them and sending them home. Now when they're with you, they are home, and without the stability you provide, there would be none.

Drugs, mental health and societal issues, incarceration, and the military have decimated our families, and grandparents who should be about living their lives are stepping up to the plate so our legacy won't be lost. In other cases, grandparents are fighting over who can do the most for the little ones, and they're generating court cases because of it. The real shame is that so many children have no parents or grandparents to spoil them or teach them the things they need to know. Hats off to you if you're taking up the slack. I know it's not easy, and I pray if you're being a grand and a parent, your joy will be double as you protect our next generation of parents and grandparents. Be encouraged.

Lord, being a grandparent is a precious gift. Help us treat every child like grandparents would. Amen.

*Children are a great comfort in one's old age, which one would
not reach so quickly if one didn't have children.*
—Unknown

4. Yes, You Can Have a Sandwich without Miracle Whip.

Scripture: Psalm 37:23-31; 1 Timothy 5:1-8

The first thing that comes to my mind when I think of sandwiches is grilled cheese on crunchy wheat bread, nicely toasted, warm and gooey. Yes, I'm having some chips that I don't need and a warm chocolate chip cookie to chase it, but for many of us the word *sandwich* brings on another set of stressful images. We're in what we know as the "sandwich generation"—raising children and caring for elderly parents and always trying to balance something that somebody needs.

Between soccer practice, ballet lessons, Mom's doctor appointments, picking up Dad's prescriptions, and making sure somebody is available to stay with Aunt Lillie, it's easy to be stressed out and about to crash with too many things to do and no help in sight. Some elderly parents are very independent and call only when they can't find any other way to manage, while others love pushing the "you don't care about me" buttons. No matter what you do, it's never enough. If your children and your parents are all under the same roof, there's never a dull moment. If they're in two or more locations, you're always going to and fro; and even when you're still, your mind's running.

An old Miracle Whip salad dressing commercial touted, "A sandwich just isn't a sandwich without Miracle Whip," but I beg to differ. This place where we find ourselves sandwiched may be a blessing *and* a curse when it comes to quality-of-life issues. Because of modern technology and medical advances, we can now be kept alive seemingly forever without knowing who or where we are—especially if we've not made our wishes known. Further, if we opt for nursing home facilities, that decision may be the topic of every subsequent family gathering. I don't know which is worse—the guilt of not having done enough for your parents or the guilt of shortchanging your children. If you consider your own personal needs, this is a "luxury" that gets lost in translation.

There are no easy answers, but here are some real truths we must consider. (1) You can't do everything, no matter how cute or strong you are—ask for help and hold others accountable. If you're the primary caregiver, work out a regular time when other family members come and help out so you can rest, go on a vacation, or do nothing except nothing. (2) Make a living will, if you haven't done

23

so already. Tell your family often what it says and where to find it. Dying with dignity beats living in a vegetative state any day. Don't have a living will? Call an attorney Monday. (3) Pick an assisted-living facility so if you're unable to live alone, you know what will happen next. (4) Before you haul anybody anywhere else, or make another appointment, turn off the phones and take a nap. (5) If your children are almost driving age, ask for a hardship license so they can handle some of the transportation chores. (6) Decrease the number of activities you get the children involved in, so you won't have so much to do. (7) Lower your housekeeping standards, and when someone asks, "Can I help?" don't be a martyr; have a list.

Listen to me: You must set limits before you're over in the corner picking imaginary lint bunnies off your clothes. You won't be able to help anyone if you have a stress-induced stroke or heart attack. Today, go make yourself a grilled cheese sandwich and a cup of tea and save your life.

Lord, I do all I can. Give me the wisdom to know when to ask for help. Amen.

The most important things in life aren't things.
—Anthony J. D'Angelo

5. Invest in Priceless.

Scripture: James 1:2-3, 16-17

I love a good television advertisement, and MasterCard has some of the best. They show you expensive restaurants and great vacations, and then they'll end with something mushy like, "Being there with the one you love—priceless." While priceless is certainly in the eye of the beholder, most of the time those moments are pretty easy to spot and they provide the boost we need to get across the finish line. The older I get, the more those priceless moments mean to me, and after my father's death three years ago, I decided to do whatever it takes to make the good times a priority.

I almost didn't stop at my parents' house that Thursday night in early September. I had run into my mother and her friend Miss Girlean earlier, and Miss Girlean urged me to stop and see my dad. When I did, I stayed about three hours and enjoyed every moment. When I got ready to leave he said, "Now Cynthie, you know your daddy loves you." I assured him I knew this with all my heart. I kissed him on the forehead, told him I loved him too, and left. That Saturday a heart attack silenced him, but our parting words keep me going.

A year earlier my parents had celebrated their fiftieth anniversary, and we had a wonderful party to honor them. Since they had not had a wedding, we worked to make this occasion special. The eight of us and our families arranged for them to be picked up in a limousine, then we rounded up their neighbors and friends and threw them a buffet dinner. Virtually everyone who came told them not just how special they were that day but how much joy they had brought us through the years. When my father said it was one of the happiest days of his life, that made it worth every effort we had made. It really was priceless.

When our daughter, Angela, finished her undergraduate degree in three years, our whole family came to the graduation. Since she was the first grandchild on either side of her family to complete this feat, we invited the elders of the family to give her a blessing and lay hands on her. We shared our dreams and hopes with her and sent her out into the world to conquer it. Look in the dictionary under *priceless* and there's a picture of us.

Our son Marcos's wedding day was also one of those priceless days. Angela was pledging her sorority, and of course that was the day she needed pinning. My sister

Adriane literally drove all over Tennessee to make the day special. She started out in Nashville, drove two hours and a half to Knoxville, pinned Angela, got back in the car, and drove six hours to Memphis for the wedding. My husband, Roger, performed the ceremony, and when he reached over and kissed Marcos on the forehead, we almost didn't get through the rest of the ceremony. Priceless.

I am blessed that in my family we all like each other, and gatherings are fun, though I know that it's not the case in every family. The tough and difficult times will come whether we are prepared for them or not, so we must seize the happy times every chance we get. Spend your money while you're alive to enjoy anniversaries, birthdays, promotions, graduations, and on and on. Don't let the only times you gather with friends and family be for sad reasons or to settle scores. Life is short, and the older I get the shorter it seems to be getting. Take time to write a note to brighten someone's day. Send a stunning bouquet to someone who is struggling with cancer or who could really use a word of encouragement. Some things you can buy, but the really good stuff replaces your money with something much more valuable. Invest in priceless today.

Lord, we count it all joy and give you the glory for the good things in life. Amen.

*Children are our future, teach them well and
let them lead the way.*
—Whitney Houston

6. And a Child Shall Lead Them.

Scripture: Matthew 7:9-11

I don't know who had the most fun at Chuck E. Cheese—Kierra or me. (It was probably me.) We were on our first date in weeks and were going out to eat and to a movie. When we couldn't decide where to go for food, she quietly said, "I've always wanted to go to Chuck E. Cheese." I was delighted, because if there's anything fifty-two-year-old kids love, it's rodents who entertain. (Think Mickey and Minnie Mouse, Mighty Mouse, and, of course, Chuck E.) If they gave me unlimited tokens, I might never go home.

Kierra and I have been together since she was in first grade. Before that I had two other little friends. I'm a mentor and, as my Friend to Friend shirt says, "a trusted friend." (I was delighted to get a little one whose name was the same as my granddaughter's—instead of a different name, I just have to keep up with the spellings.) Kierra and I talk about all kinds of stuff, and I visit her school when I can get the time off. I was honored and humbled when she wanted to take me to the free minor league baseball game she won as a gift for good grades.

Neither of us had ever been to a ball game before, and after we got there we discovered that her coupon had expired. We were all dressed up for a ball game, so we were going to see a ball game one way or the other. We went in and ate pizza, burgers, cotton candy, popcorn—in short, junk and lots of it. I knew her mother would call me at 3:00 a.m. and give me a good chewing out. Thank goodness everything stayed down. Kierra and I had the best time, and I decided that night that I would always want to be a mentor.

Even before I knew the word *mentors,* I had them. When I was a child, Opal and her older brothers James, Edward, and Jimmy Louis lived next door, and they took time with me. Opal let me ramble in her purse, and when she went off to college she sent me letters—and if there's anything little kids love, it's getting mail. Mickey, who lived farther down the road, would tell me about the facts of life and give me her hand-me-downs. I loved it.

I guess I've mentored informally all my life too, but about seven years ago I got involved formally. I said in a speech at a local church that I'd like to do some mentoring, and before I left the room I had my chance. The first program was called PAL. I can't remember what it stood for, but I was proud to go have lunch with my little one every week. When we moved to Jackson, I got Kierra and we've been friends and best buds ever since. She's given me lots of funny stories and insights, and she translates kid-speak for me. I love watching her grow into a beautiful young woman. Her honesty is refreshing—one day after I'd been to the barber shop she took one look and said, "You look like a boy!"

I know now if you don't want the truth and stark honesty, don't ask little kids because they will call a spade just what it is—a darned old shovel. They will also love you boldly and unconditionally. If you want to do something important with your life, consider being a mentor. It takes only as much time as you have to give, but the benefits multiply exponentially. Certainly you can give stuff, but your time and attention mean more and that's the thing you will both remember.

Lord, we know you love the children. Help us today to love and care for them as well. Help us keep them safe and let them know you through seeing you in us. Amen.

Every queen needs her own castle.
—Alvis Marie Bond

7. Nesting Is for Birds, Not Children.

Scripture: Ephesians 5:31; Luke 15:11-31

I love my children and they are two of the nicest people I know, but when they turned eighteen I encouraged them strongly to be about their lives, whether that meant college, the military, or both. I laugh and tell people that Marcos and Angela have been gone for more than ten years, and I work full-time to keep them gone. I love having my husband, and my home, free of people I gave birth to.

Erma Bombeck is often credited with saying, "Never let someone you gave birth to drive your car." That may need to be altered to read "Be cautious about adult children who are on their way to whatever it is they intend to become and just need to stay at your house while they figure it out." Frankly, there's not that much figuring to do.

When our daughter suggested living with us for a year to get established in her law practice, I volunteered to get a part-time job to help her pay rent someplace else. The thought of her bringing in all her stuff from college and trying to keep track of her whereabouts didn't sound like fun.

Our son, whose midnight curfew didn't suit him well after he turned eighteen, would wake me up at 2:30 a.m. to tell me he was at somebody else's house. I'm suspecting he knew his plans at midnight but thought better about calling while I was alert enough to question him. He knew that once I went to sleep there would be few questions. The combination of trying to give him freedom and getting uninterrupted sleep was a real challenge.

When the opportunity to send them both off to college at the same time presented itself, I was almost giddy, because as long as you're at my home you are *my* child and I want to keep parenting you. It doesn't matter how old you are or how much freedom you think you're supposed to have now that you're grown.

Some parents and adult children can live together harmoniously, but I believe unless there is some serious discussion or reason, cultural or otherwise, adults need their own roof. When I was growing up I could hardly wait to move out and have a job, a car, and my own castle so I could do "everything I was big enough to do," as old folks used to say. I could just taste being grown-up.

Nowadays, lounging around at home forever seems to

be the norm—anything you're big enough to do, you can do at home with your parents. Household rules have fallen by the way, and we have made home such a comfortable place that nobody wants to leave. But we may be doing our children a disservice by not making them pay part of the utilities, the food bill, the mortgage, something. It's called responsibility. You don't need the money? Fine—give it to charity or put it in an account for them, but at least make sure they pay some part of their own way.

Parenting is a big job, and part of our work is to give our children roots and wings. We've got the first piece figured out; it's the letting go that seems to have us stumped. Watching our babies go into an uncertain world is one of the hardest things we will ever have to do, but we can learn from the father in Luke 15, who knew that with God's help his son would come back older and wiser. Our children can too. Eagles prepare their eaglets to fly and then push them from the nests. The eaglets become great flyers, knowing that their parents are there to catch them if they fall. Let's prepare, push, cheer, and get some sleep.

Lord, help me let go of my children when it's time, for my sake and theirs. Guard, protect, and strengthen them as they flex their wings. Amen.

Shop till you drop.
—Author's recreation mantra

8. I'd Rather Be Shopping.

Scripture: Matthew 7:7-12

I call the first Tuesday in December my retail therapy day. I go to the mall at opening time and stay until it closes. I go early so I can park right outside the store where I think I will finish. Then I visit every store, unlike during regular times when I zip in one store and back out. I listen to the music, admire the displays, have some lunch and cookies, watch the other shoppers shop, and leisurely enjoy the season.

Since stores created gift cards, I feel free not to figure out if someone would like the fuzzy robe or the frilly one or if the jogging suit is hip enough. I go alone and take my time. (I haven't found anyone who can last past 5:02 p.m. without wanting to leave me and my packages on the curb.)

My husband asks, "What in the world do you do at the mall all day?" I tell him what I told you and he still doesn't understand. He, like most people, wants to go, pick up a few things, and call it a day. Because of the convenience, some people actually prefer shopping online. I, on the other hand, don't want to sit at my computer and wonder what the blouse feels like. I don't want to take off my clothes and try it on, but I certainly want to touch it, and it matters not if I visit fifteen other stores and then go back and buy the first thing I looked at. That's why I call it therapy—I work at my own pace.

Shopping satisfies me because I separate it from spending. I shop because I enjoy it and I've already calculated how much I can and want to spend. Unfortunately, in many circles, television shopping, tons of maxed-out credit cards, and personal unhappiness are turning *shopping* into a bad word. One Macy's clerk said that working in her department was tough because she wants all the cute things that come in. If I worked there, that might be my problem too.

Another acquaintance almost went down the financial drain after she got addicted to the networks that bring shopping a few channel clicks away. Television and movies are filled with people who go shopping and spend thousands when they're depressed or trying to make themselves feel better. I have discovered that money, in all its forms, is an interesting thing—you've got to have it to function, but with it comes an enormous and serious responsibility. Advertisements tell us that we can buy happiness with card A or B, and when we run short, we can get a loan and keep spending.

Don't believe the hype. Credit and money are wonderful, but you have to manage them or they manage you. One year my American Express bill, on which I ordinarily paid the balance every month, offered me an opportunity to "roll over" my purchases in excess of two hundred dollars. Sounded great. The next thing I knew, my balance looked like the national debt and was on its way to being unmanageable. When I looked at the interest rate, I knew I had to do something or I'd have to live to be a thousand just to pay this one bill. I got a part-time job, put every penny toward eliminating the bill, and vowed not to go that route again.

I can't tell you how to spend your money, but I can advise you to spend some, save some, and share some, and when you set part of it aside for fun, spend only that. Pay your credit card balances every month, and only charge what you can pay in full. Pay more than the minimum balance, and if you're spending your whole check to pay your credit card bills—unless you're using it for points or cash back or are getting it interest-free— please reevaluate your strategy. Don't be a slave to credit, debt, or money. Use them wisely, and if you're looking for me in December, start at Macy's and work your way to the cookies.

Lord, help us be responsible with our gifts and seek your will in all that we do. Amen.

*You better not try to stand in my way as I'm walking
out the door.*
—*Johnny Paycheck*

9. Take This Job and Shove It.

Scripture: Luke 15:15-19

If I have to work, and I do, I believe I'm supposed to enjoy it. If my work makes my head hurt just to get up and go, I find something else to do. When I was teaching, I urged my students on the first day of classes to make me do my best work. I told them, "You need to learn, and it is my job to teach. If I don't work, don't pay me, and I need my pay, so make me work."

They'd snicker, but around midterm I'd ask, "So, how am I doing? What do you like? What don't you like? What can I do to make the class better?" I'd ask them to type their honest answers into the computer anonymously, and I'd fix what I could and incorporate suggestions for the next time. I usually ignored the ones about the amount of homework—trust me, if they had too much homework, I would have been the first to know because

I'd be drowning in papers every night. Each year I gave myself a ten-thousand-dollar raise because I loved my work, and over the years I got pretty good. (Mind you, this was imaginary money, but it made me feel better.)

I told my students that I'd had enough bad jobs to know a good one when I saw it, and that was the truth. I had whined and moaned through at least three jobs I can name, and as the saying goes, "If Mama ain't happy, ain't nobody happy." Roger begged me to quit those jobs, because he couldn't take the constant complaining. I was underemployed but my employer didn't agree, and my head hurt every morning when it was time to go to work. The closer I got to the office, the more it hurt, and by lunch it was ugly. By the time I got home, if the world hadn't ended, I was complaining about my work.

That's no way to live, and if your boss is a conehead and micromanages, it will drive you to drinking, and at fifty-two I'm entirely too old and too cheap to take up drinking. (I'm not old; I'm just too old to start something so serious.)

A few years back I had one of "those" days at work, and if I had been a quitter, Johnny Paycheck and I both would've been singing his song. I not only wanted to say, "Shove it," I had a pointy-toed pair of fuchsia heels ready to get the process started.

I prayed, and the Lord spoke quickly and reminded me that I was where I was because it had been ordained for me to be there. I didn't know the Reverend Robert Felder well at the time, but his words probably would have helped me make the decision not just to stay but to stay, play, and win. When his younger brother Luther had a tough challenge, Robert reminded him, "Son, that ain't no distance for a stepper." Translated for me it said, "If you can't stand a little heat in the kitchen, how will you make delicious lemon pound cake, lemon tarts, creamy lemon pie, and lemon cookies from your lemons?"

I did something about my situation, and you must too. Bad work, too much work, nasty coworkers—all these things shorten your life. That pain in your neck? Stress. Those chest pains? Probably the same thing. During my tenure process I learned that my irregular heartbeat and other new symptoms had all been brought on by the stress. I vowed I would never again let my work send me to that place.

I'm begging you: Don't let your work do it to you. Think about all the talents you have and start your own business. Use your networks, and let your friends know you are job hunting. (Most of them already know because you've been whining for some time now.) Whoever said, "If you find work you love, you'll never work another day in your life," knew we'd come along and need some encouragement. Do it today: Find that something that makes your heart sing, that something that you'd do for free. The money will follow.

Lord, help us find work that glorifies you and makes us sing. Amen.

Every family tree produces some nuts.
—Unknown

10. Family Traditions.
11. And Such.

Scripture: Matthew 1:1-17

Every time I read about Jesus and his "begat" generations, I think back to my own family and wonder if Jesus had relatives like Aunt Florence and Aunt Velma and Uncle Willie, who always make me feel like the smartest, most beautiful niece in the world. We know Jesus was smart, so I'm figuring they kissed him on the cheeks and bragged about him to their friends. I can only imagine what they said after the wedding when he turned water into wine. Jesus probably even had an uncle who would come see his little brother Joseph and bring his grandchildren to play, like my Uncle Bud did.

Uncle Bud had an award-winning smile, and he and my father loved to laugh and seemed to enjoy each other's company immensely. I'm figuring Jesus' grandmother was probably like my grandmother Clara, who was always handy when her husband needed help tying something up with the equivalent of today's duct tape. She probably kept cold biscuits in the cabinet, told funny stories, and repeated Bible verses. I know his cousins came to Bethlehem or Jerusalem to spend summers.

It doesn't say that Jesus' parents had to chop and pick cotton, but I'll wager that like my parents, they had to handle the livestock so they didn't get out and root up the neighbor's fig trees and wheat fields. One day I stopped at my parents' house and I knocked and knocked but nobody came to the door. I was puzzled because the automobile inventory indicated they were home. As I was about to leave, I heard my name and saw my dad waving from his hog pen next door. I found him and my mother penned up with the biggest, orneriest looking sows and some of the cutest little pigs I had ever seen.

My parents were trying to separate the mothers from the little ones because the little ones kept slipping out and rooting up Miss Carrie's flowers. The mamas weren't happy. Not one bit. My father had some kind of instrument to control them, and my mother was trying feverishly to contain the pigs, watch the mamas, and do what Dad needed her to do amidst a million squeals. Most important, she was trying to stay alive. The two of them looked up at me and we all fell out laughing. I made a fast getaway because they obviously didn't have time to visit. I'm figuring Joseph and Mary had similar challenges.

Our families come in all shapes and sizes and they

41

make us who we are. I am blessed to have seven siblings and they are some of the nicest people I know, and I'm not the only one who says it. They're smart and funny and we are so blessed to have had an awesome extended family—terrific grandparents, phenomenal aunts and uncles, beautiful and talented cousins. When I was growing up, our house, my grandparents' house next door, and Auntie's house were always exciting places to be.

Someone interesting always dropped in, and they'd delight us with their adventures in the military or in the cities where I longed to live. We'd stay up late, laughing and telling jokes, and during the summer we'd swat flies and mosquitoes and revel in the fun times. Much of what we learned came from hanging around outside the windows and around the porches and listening when we were supposed to be playing but weren't. When the adults said, "Go outside and play," that was our cue to move out of sight because juicy gossip was about to be imparted. Of course once we heard it, we had to spread the word.

Other stories were deliberately shared to teach lessons. I am convinced that the lessons and stories are why our neighborhoods and families thrived—without them we would have been lost, with no direction. Our ancestors modeled the behaviors we either wanted to emulate or to avoid at all costs.

Roger, my husband, tells how his grandfather Isaiah, called "Daddy," always taught him and his brothers to provide for their families. Daddy told them his family had been sharecroppers, and his father let the landowner take all their sustenance, and so the family didn't have anything to eat. That made such an impression on Roger that rarely does he come home without bringing some food to make sure we don't starve. Every time we move, somebody remarks about how much food we keep on hand. We have Isaiah Goodlow to thank.

Anytime I want inspiration for my educational journey, I look back at my grandmother Orelia, who earned her GED when she was fifty-six. She worked so hard on her education and never stopped preaching, "Get an education so you can be somebody." She corrected our southern twang and informal language and let us know that it was never all right to be outside our home with rollers in our hair or to be in any way inappropriately dressed. Years after she died I was doing an interview with a woman who had gone to church with her, and the woman talked about how beautifully presented my grandmother always was. I never forget that whether I'm running to the store at midnight or noon, Orelia is watching.

Uncle James and Uncle Nelson were war heroes and many of their medals and accolades have gotten lost, but we keep telling what little we know. Uncle James lied about his age to get into the military, and as a medic Uncle Nelson saved lives during his enlistment. My father had military stories of his own, and he used them to convince youngsters not to get hooked on

43

drugs. Though my father was smart and talented enough to get ahead on his own, he told the youngsters how he got promoted sooner than usual when some of the people in front of him went down in flames because of their addictions.

Sharing our family's legacy is critical—when we know we come from a great people, it gives us permission to be great too. If we think nobody cares about excellence, we may settle for "all right." The stories of hard times are often so painful that we have filed them way away, never to be remembered, but every experience contains a lesson, and no experience is wasted if we learn from it.

Nowadays, with our families in shambles and our communities being taken over by thugs, stories are more important than ever. Some stories are embarrassing and others are inspirational, but they're all a part of who we are. We must write them down and tell them every chance we get. My children hated it when they would ask what seemed like a simple question and then got a whole trunk full of information they never asked for. If we were riding in the car, I had a captive audience and used it to their advantage, though they didn't always see it that way. Every once in a while, though, they'd come back and ask for some clarification to get the story right, and I knew they had heard.

We must keep our family trees up-to-date and record the stories of the elders while they are still lucid. Better yet, let the young ones in your family do the questioning and recording. They need to know how they were begotten and by whom. With knowledge comes power, and with power comes might. Let's be strong and mighty.

Lord, because of our families and our heritage we are great and grateful. Amen.

Going to the chapel and we're gonna get married—not!
—Author

12. The Tombstone Won't Say, "She Never Married."

Scripture: Proverbs 14:1, 7; 16:1-3

Even before Ken and Barbie drove off in her pink convertible, I wanted to find a fairy-tale prince, get married, and live happily ever after. I wanted him to be tall, dark, and handsome, and if he happened to be rich, that would've been frosting on my beautifully decorated princess cake. I figured that I'd have to kiss a few frogs along the way, but I knew there was a prince out there somewhere with a size-seven glass slipper. (OK, this was a long time ago—I didn't know my feet would grow when I had children and got stout.)

My friends and I had picked out some cute guys from high school to marry, and we talked about how much weddings cost and we cheered for the people on television who got married, but we never dwelt much on if or when it would actually happen. If a friend married somebody cute, we wanted to know if he had brothers. Today that seems to be the $64,000 question—not just does he have brothers, but do his cousins have brothers, do his coworkers have brothers, does anybody have brothers who could come to marry some of our land's fair maidens?

Unfortunately, the statistics aren't offering much hope. Recent studies show that huge numbers of women are unmarried, have never been married, and probably won't marry. The Marines and some single women now share the same goal: finding a few good men. College women are outnumbering college men by as much as two to one, which makes finding Mr. Right fairly unlikely. Thank goodness many women are single by choice, are already in committed relationships, or live happily without frogs or princes.

Sadly, some of our best and brightest men are languishing in prison, homeless shelters, and drug rehab centers because of poor mental health, bad credit, foolish choices, and drugs. Many of them have given in to hopelessness and despair.

So, what's a woman who wants marriage to do? I have ten comments and suggestions I'd like to offer. (I know you're thinking the last thing you need is a fiftyish woman who hasn't been single in over thirty years giving advice to singles, but indulge me because I know stuff.)

1. Remember, you are a complete person with or without a man.

2. Bask in who you are and understand that your worth isn't tied to whether you marry or not.

3. If your biological clock is ticking loudly, adopt, mentor, do foster care, or borrow a niece or nephew to spoil.

4. Honor the person God has made you, knowing that if and when God sends you a mate, your chances for being equally yoked will improve.

5. If you treat yourself with respect and dignity, then everyone else will. This means that you don't have to settle for a lying, cheating, nonworking, bad-credit, lay-around-the-house-and-take-up-all-the-air kind of fellow, because, contrary to what some people say, a piece of a man is *not* better than no man. Protect yourself in every way.

6. No matter how cute he is or how lonely you are, do not consider sharing a married man—if he cheats on her, eventually he will cheat on you too.

7. Treasure your friends who keep you focused on the positives in your life.

8. Look for compatibility, potential, and dreams, not material things.

9. Don't even think of hanging out at funeral homes trolling for grieving widowers. Give them time to figure out which end is up, even if Sister So-and-So is over there the next day with her famous chicken casserole.

10. Verify. If something doesn't feel right, listen and ask questions.

If things work out, call me. If not, return the talking frogs for a full refund.

Lord, remind me that I can be complete in you. You know my heart and your will for my life—please prepare me for whatever you have in store. Amen.

If I can help somebody . . . then my living shall not be in vain.
—Alma B. Androzzo

13. You Can Ring My Bell.

Scripture: Galatians 6:2-10

I can't remember when I began ringing the Salvation Army bell during the Thanksgiving and Christmas holidays, but I do it religiously and have way more fun than I'm supposed to. It all started when I responded to a request for volunteers in our local paper and culminated in my being named the Jackson, Tennessee, Individual Bell Ringer of the Year, a designation I treasure but one I didn't need in order to be inspired to ring, ring, ring. I do it because I love seeing what happens when everybody pitches in.

Most people are happy to put something in the bright red kettle if they have it. When they say, "All I've got is change," I rejoice and remind them that when their change meets their neighbor's change, we can change the world. They buy it every time. Over the years I've made sure that I affirm parents who share and teach their children to share. Saying "Thank you and God bless you" to each donor brings a smile from even the busiest shopper, and I am always humbled when someone responds by saying "God bless you, too."

After ringing that bell for two hours, you can pretty well hear ringing in your sleep or at other, inconvenient waking moments. One day the imaginary ringing came in handy when the captain passed the kettle along but forgot to leave a bell. Everyone who donated on that December day giggled and teased me about the invisible bell I rang.

Bell ringing isn't for everyone. You bundle up beyond recognition, pace to stay warm, and stand in one place for two hours; and the Lord knows that not everyone has the temperament or the inclination to meet and greet harried shoppers. Fret not; there's a volunteer opportunity out there with your name on it. You just have to name and claim it.

Several of my friends volunteer at local hospitals, getting free checkups and other perks, while others organize or run in charity events such as Race for the Cure. I used to do the American Heart Association's Neighbor-to-Neighbor Campaign so I could meet people when I moved to a new neighborhood. I was embarrassed that I didn't know my neighbors' names and couldn't recognize them at the store if they didn't identify themselves. Trust me, there's nothing that'll bring you closer than showing up at somebody's house and asking for money. I was always warmly received.

I am passionate about volunteering, but four years ago I realized that my passion was getting lost in "busyness." One sunny day I realized that if volunteering was important to me, and it was, then I had to let go of stuff that I didn't care about but that required a lot of attention. It was then that I stopped letting people put me on committees that have lots of meetings. Now I say up front, "I don't do meetings. If there's something you need me to do, tell me what it is and if I can, I'll be glad to, but I don't do meetings."

I am happy to report that in the past four years, not one organization has folded because I didn't come to meetings. I meet all the time at work, so the last thing I want to do when I'm not working is go to another meeting. Besides, I can't ring bells, meet new neighbors, or do the stuff I want to do if I'm sitting in a meeting.

Look for me outside the local Kroger or Macy's, where my bell and I will be doing our thing. Won't you help?

Time is precious and scarce, Lord. Help me use mine in making the world better. Amen.

Anyone who thinks the sky is the limit has limited imagination.
—Unknown

14. Nothing Shall Be Impossible— That Definitely Includes Statistics.

Scripture: Mark 11:22-24; Hebrews 10:35–11:6

The Scriptures were clear: "Believe that you have received it, and it will be yours." But that's where the problem came in. I didn't believe I had received it. "It" was math aptitude. I had signed up for and dropped Algebra II three times in undergraduate school. I finally muddled through with a C after my professor had mercy on me, possibly because she felt sorry for my tutor, whom I had worn to a frazzle by semester's end.

Then came the statistics class. I kept telling myself, "I am not stupid. I can do this." But in my heart all I could hear was my teacher's voice telling me, "Now little girl, your sister could get this work," and all I could feel were his switches on my legs in front of my seventh-grade class when I couldn't work the problems. I was traumatized, though I didn't know the word then, and I grew to hate math. I worked around my math trauma as much as possible, but the doctoral-level statistics—well, that was a horse of a different color. There was nowhere to run and nowhere to hide, and trust me, I looked. I signed up for statistics twice, and I dropped out twice, unable to do the work.

I bought some self-help books and finally realized that, no, I wasn't stupid—my foundation was weak. It was like I was building a house but putting the roof on first, which explained why the walls and floors kept crumbling.

I had no choice but to pray. A lot. That summer I signed up for the statistics class a third time, figuring the third time's the charm, or so the adage goes. I asked everybody who would/could/did pray regularly to pray for me and my professor by name. Between their prayers and my listening to Aretha Franklin classics to and from class, the Lord delivered me. One of my classmates was a young woman who loved statistics, and she plopped down right beside me. She explained the gory details that I missed. Best of all, the veteran professor used familiar illustrations so the numbers finally made sense.

For me it was math, but fears and "impossibilities" come in all shapes and sizes. They can travel by car, train, plane, or bus. For you, they may look like the national teachers exam or that licensing test for cosmetology, nursing, or real estate that you keep missing by two points—never the same two points, but two points nevertheless! Maybe your fears involve public speaking, or a venture you've launched and can't move to the next level.

Whatever the fears and "impossiblities" are for you, don't give in and don't give up. God can help you conquer your fears—the real and the imagined ones. I keep a plaque on my table to remind me "never, never, never give up." The Scriptures say nothing is impossible with God, and that means absolutely, positively *no thing.* We can pray, trust, and let go. The trust part is usually the hardest for me because I want to see some evidence right away, but that's not always how God works. My church choir sings "Right Now, God Is Working It Out," and the part I love best says, "He's got your petitions, yes, and his grace is so sufficient."

No truer words were ever written. God's timing is always perfect, though it may not mesh with ours. Sometimes we want to treat our prayers the way we do an elevator—keep pushing the button so it comes sooner. What we can be sure of is that God is always listening and we really are more than conquerors. Let's live like it.

Lord, there are so many things coming at us right now, and it is easier to be overwhelmed and fearful than fully confident that you really are working things out for us. Keep our doubts and fears far from us so we can see you at work in everything that concerns us. Amen.

Don't look down on a man unless you're picking him up.
—The Jackson Southernaires

15. Dignity: It's Your Right.

Scripture: Luke 16:19-31; Matthew 25:31-46

One of the most painful scenes in *Cinderella Man,* the Russell Crowe Depression-era movie about boxing champ Jim Braddock, comes when Braddock is about to lose everything. He can't find work and has turned over every stone, almost literally, to provide for his family. He finally has to go to his friends for help. Many of them look as if they don't want to be seen with him, while others shift their eyes uncomfortably and mumble under their breath. They throw him a few dollars but not before making him feel small, dejected, and worthless.

That scene haunts me every time I exit the Interstate and see the empty-eyed men, women, and pets with the battered signs that say "Homeless, will work for food" or "Vietnam vet, hungry and homeless. Anything will help.

God bless you." I'm always torn between "Do I give money or buy food?" and "Is this really helping?" I think about what it must've taken to come, stand in the elements all day, and have people yell and curse at you. Sure, some of it may be a scam, but I believe if we've crafted a place where begging like this beats an honest day's living, the shame is on us, not them.

In another movie, *Resurrecting the Champ,* again about boxing, a reporter has discovered a homeless man who claims to be an ex-champion. Wanting to write an article about him, the reporter says he'd like to look through the man's shopping cart so he can share with his readers what the man's treasures are. The homeless man quickly replies, "Sure, and then I'll come home with you and go through your drawers and closets to see what you've got." Only then does the reporter understand that he has forgotten that this is an individual, a real human being, not just a front-page story.

Unfortunately we don't always think about how we treat one another. We just presume and assume that everyone has a job or some other means of support, somewhere safe and warm to sleep, healthy self-esteem, clean clothes, and comfortable shoes. It ain't necessarily so. Circumstances come, jobs go, mental and physical diseases invade our bodies—so many things can throw us into a tailspin and then, depending on how long the spin lasts, everything we know may be gone or changed.

I was so proud of my sister Linda, who celebrated her

fiftieth birthday by sponsoring the weekly meal her church provides at the homeless shelter. She took extreme care in selecting a special menu, and she warmly greeted each guest with dignity and respect. I wasn't surprised by her gesture, since my parents taught and lived lessons of service often enough for us to know them by heart. They showed us how to look people in the eye and how to treat everybody with dignity and respect. They said if you're down, keep your head up and don't stay down.

Sadly, some of those lessons of compassion, respect, and grace have gotten lost in our culture of "busyness" and "haves and have nots." Let's consider: When we share our expertise, office space, or talents with our brothers and sisters, do they feel ten feet tall or like shower scum? Are we giving away messages of hope along with our good suits? Can we make a difference if we start an empowerment program or a dream fund?

I say let's plant seeds of dignity and hope and help them grow. Hope reminds us the sun will come up tomorrow. Hope whispers, "Don't give up." Let's be our brothers' and sisters' keepers so we can all live our lives with dignity and honor, strength and courage, whether that means lending a hand, a dollar, or a dream. It's what God has called us to do.

Lord, open our eyes to see the hurt and pain in the world so we can show your love in all the places you would send us. Amen.

They smile in your face, all the time
they want to take your place.
—The O'Jays

16. Backstabbers Hurt Your Heart Too.

Scripture: Matthew 5:38-48

Bobby and I went back more than thirty years, all the way to before those ugly choir dresses he made us buy at Ross United Methodist Church. They were a funky mauve color, and even though my size ten fit all right, most of them fit like a sausage sack. Roger kept asking, "Why are you all letting Bobby choose the dresses you wear for the concert?" Of course I didn't have a good answer, or any other kind for that matter.

I always did what Bobby said. If he called while I was working on a major project or had a serious deadline, I stopped doing my work and did his. He was like that— you couldn't tell him no, and the Lord knows I and many others had tried. He knew that whatever he asked, if he needed me I would come through because he was my friend and I treasured him.

That Sunday morning when he called, I knew something was wrong. He said, "Why didn't you tell me you didn't like the banquet? I heard you ran down the program booklet, the speaker, the music, everything. I thought we were friends." I was devastated, because we *were* friends and I didn't know what he was talking about. I finally dragged the details out of him. At the previous night's event, a woman we both knew had sat at my table and later had given him an account of what she said had happened.

I was furious because not only had she lied about me, she was about to jeopardize a precious friendship. I said, "Bobby, you know me well enough to realize that if I had had an issue, I would've told you myself." I had barely spoken to this woman during the meal, and Bobby and I concluded that the thoughts she conveyed had been her own. My first mind was to find and body slam her like they do on television wrestling shows. Thankfully I resisted, and after an honest assessment of what had actually transpired, Bobby and I decided we would avoid Miss Sister like a dead skunk in the middle of the road.

Writing about this four years later, it still makes me sad that two-faced people like her wreak havoc in our lives with their lies, innuendoes, and rumors. Bobby and I were blessed that we had a bond of trust and that he didn't settle for her word; instead, he called and we talked. She was an acquaintance we could avoid, but oftentimes the betrayals come from deep and close within—from family, colleagues, and people we consider real friends.

Betrayal can cause some of our deepest hurts, and the scars may last a lifetime. Every time somebody or something knocks us down, it takes longer to get up and get back in the saddle, but we can and we must. Our lives are enriched by our friendships and other relationships, and the only way not to get hurt is not to get close to people or allow them to get close to you. That would be a pretty lonely way to live. As a result, I have concluded that I'd rather press forward in hope than retreat in fear that it might happen again. Of course, nothing is guaranteed except God's unconditional love and acceptance, and that's worth shouting about.

Lord, turning the other cheek when we have been betrayed and hurt is difficult. Please help us do it and forgive as you would. Amen.

It is far better to forgive and forget than to hate and remember.
—Unknown

17. I'm Sorry, So Sorry.

Scripture: Mark 11:22-26

For the record, here is a disclaimer: I am not mean, nasty, or vindictive, but when you mess with the folks I love, my first reaction has nothing to do with what Jesus would do. Maybe that's why I never bought one of those WWJD bracelets. At times like that, I know God would not be pleased at what I'm thinking. As a matter of fact, I would have a hard time trying to get in the pearly gates dragging that burden on my back.

I have offered to call "Guido and the boys" to straighten one friend's fiancé out, to help another's husband come to his senses, and to settle some other lingering scores. (I admit I don't know anybody named Guido, but I watch lots of gangster movies and they've always got a "Guido" who loves to break bones, especially arms and legs.) The real truth is that forgiveness is a lot harder than calling imaginary guys named Guido. Mustering up the strength and courage to wipe someone's slate clean when they have done us wrong takes God moving all around us and within us. Saying "I'm sorry" may be harder than bearing children, mining coal, chopping cotton, or building railroads, and accepting it and letting go of a grudge is even harder. But until you say the words and let go of the hatred and anger that sears your soul and rots your bones, you can't move forward.

Victims of crime and molestation are scarred for life, and yet forgiveness is a key piece of their healing. Suffering in silence gives the criminal and molester power long after the dastardly deed is done. In marriages and relationships, betrayal and deception can destroy the fragile bonds of trust, and rock us to the core.

One of my friends confided that she had done everything humanly possible to be a good wife, and still her husband cheated. She had kept Victoria's Secret and Frederick's of Hollywood in business and thought she had the perfect marriage. Then she discovered that not only was he engaged in an extramarital affair, it was not a one-night fling as she had hoped but a long-term, firmly entrenched romance with someone she knew. She asked, "How can I ever trust him or any man again?" I asked if she loved him more than she hated the thought of him cheating. After she got past the embarrassment and hurt, she admitted that she did, but she still didn't know if she could forgive him and forget what he had done. I told her that, unfortunately, forgiveness and forgetfulness come in the same package. Like soft lemon ice cream and warm lemon pound cake, peanut butter and jelly, spaghetti and meatballs—you can have one without the other, but it doesn't go down as easily.

Holding on to the hurt is your right. It may even make you feel better for a while, but the wound can never heal until you forgive, whether the person who wronged you asks or not. It takes a big person to say "I'm sorry," but that's where we start, and it takes someone who is bigger and better to accept. Don't let grudges, hurt, and shame keep you a prisoner any longer—forgive, let it go, and be whole again.

If you can't just yet and you still need Guido's number, call me. My prayer is that you won't need him or the boys.

Forgive us, Lord, as we forgive those who have hurt us and caused us pain. Erase the deeds from our hearts and minds so we can be free. Amen.

Everything must change, nothing stays the same. . . .
The young become the old and mysteries do unfold.
—Oleta Adams

18. Change Belongs in Your Pocket.

Scripture: Psalm 25:1-15

You gotta know when to hold 'em, know when to fold 'em, know when to walk away, and know when to run." I'm haunted by these profound words from the Kenny Rogers hit "The Gambler." I have just given up my tenured faculty position at a university where I taught for ten and a half years. The day I went to clear out my office was terrible. I came to my comic-strip-covered door; went inside; saw the pictures of my students, the plaques that kept me inspired through my dissertation and tenure process, and gifts from my friends; and I wept. And wept.

It was home, and I had spent many hours behind those doors. When I was a young professor I had even spent a couple of restless nights in those two ugly orange chairs. Always, though, I had enjoyed my work. I told the department chair that I felt guilty taking my pay because it didn't seem like work. (Mind you, I took the money and spent it, but I felt guilty.) As I touched everything on my desk and thumbed through my teaching notes and examples, I thought about the privilege I had been given to teach. My students are doing well in newspapers, television, magazines, all kinds of places, and they still call.

Then the song's lyrics hit me. I always wanted to know when to go. And though it was difficult, this was a good time to try something new. I finally got every paper, paper clip, and file, closed the door, and left. I'm leaving by choice, saying good-bye on my own terms, and that, too, is a privilege.

I'm changing. So is my job, the area where I live, the way I work, everything. I've chosen to change, but sometimes we don't get that option. A television commercial says, "Life comes at you fast," and it does. Change is inevitable and fluid. It's like catching chickens. I grew up on a farm, and during the summer our city cousins would come and relentlessly chase our poor chickens. At first the chickens were slow and looked like an easy catch, but as soon as the children got close and thought they had one, the chickens changed speed or direction. The most those kids ever got was a few feathers. As with life, as soon as we think we've figured it out, things change.

Sometimes death brings change, and when it comes unexpectedly, much of what we meant to say gets silenced forever. Circumstances and administrations change and bring opportunities for growth if we're willing to take a chance. Other times we wallow and languish in regret for a line that got crossed and can never be uncrossed. We're fascinated by change but often paralyzed by it too. Then fear moves in—fear of the unknown, of the familiar, of the possibilities, or just plain fear. And yet God calls us to move on.

Your change may be prompted by the death of a spouse. I read about a woman whose husband died years ago, and his clothes are still hanging where he left them, and she's as raw now as she was that sad April day. I can understand that, because grief will cripple you if you let it. Don't let it. Get back out into creation, and live like you mean it.

Change will come, and the best we can hope for is that we have authored and initiated it, because then we get to decide whether or how we'll play the hand we've been dealt. My prayer is that you will be blessed no matter which choice you make.

I am yours, Lord. Direct me to new paths as I courageously move forward. Amen.

Grandma's daddy didn't like me none but I loved
your Grandma so.
—Collin Raye

19. Gotta Have In-laws So We Can Have Country Music.

Scripture: Ruth 1:18

I think they created in-laws just so they'd have some-thing to write about in country music. It seems like it's the father-in-law who doesn't like the li'l scruffy fellow the daughter brings home, or it's the mother-in-law who's built like a brick house and that makes Susie Jean or Becky Sue, pick one, such a fine young woman in those blue jeans. I admit I probably listen to too much country music, but you can pretty well figure those song-writers either have really good or really bad in-laws. Or after listening, maybe the term ought to be outlaws.

I have had to bite my tongue when I tried to help my chil-dren pick a mate who seemed "so sweet" or had "such a kind heart." Their stock reply, "Mama, you just don't know (fill in the blank) like I do," kept me quiet. My first thought was "And you know what else? I don't think I ever want to know them like that either." In-laws, those folks you inherit when you get married or when your siblings get married, come in all shapes, sizes, and personalities. Some you have to work at liking, while others you adore at first sight.

There's an old adage that says if you want to know what your wife will look like in thirty years, look at her mother. Roger told me he was betting on that being true, and he's been blessed because the older my mom gets, the more beautiful she is. But I say you ought to pause and look at a bunch of things—family habits, rules, extended kin—before you get too far in love.

I have wonderful in-laws, thank God, and they have been that way from the first day—almost. Roger's Uncle Nelson was the only person I allowed to call me "Cindy" and get a reply. He loved me dearly, but I wasn't so sure the first time Roger took me home. "Uncle" took one look at me and fell out laughing. I was unnerved, but we became fast buddies and he made sure Roger always walked the line. I love him still, even though he's been gone more than twenty years.

Roger warned me that his mother was tough on girls he brought home. He had a long list of those she didn't like, and considering he was her oldest, I understood. I was relieved when she indicated that I had passed the "I think I like her" test. My sisters- and brothers-in-law are a fine bunch too, and I am blessed, unlike some of my friends, who got some real coneheads in the deal, as well as some sibling rivalry.

69

Let me show you: When my friend brought a dozen roses for the mother, the sister-in-law brought two. When nobody ate this brother's wife's squash casserole, she left the mom's house walking. Here's a better one: Son A's wife bought the father some shoes, but Son's B's wife worked at a shoe store, and since Son A's wife didn't buy them from her, they didn't speak for months. Confusion, mayhem, and jockeying for position make family gatherings an adventure, if not a living hell.

According to the advice columns, if your in-laws don't like you, there's not much you can do about it (except write a country song, of course). I took my son and his fiancé to lunch the day before their wedding and gave them a cute little book of lessons that I had learned during my marriage. I told them everything I needed to say, such as keep other folks out of your business, love and trust each other, take the children to church, always talk to and not at each other, and then I assured them I was going to do what my mother-in-law did: mind my own business. If you can handle things early and not allow them to simmer, if you can make sure everybody's clear about expectations and can mind your own business, chances are you can make your marriage work...and have some great song lyrics too, if you feel like singing.

For my family, Lord, thank you. For the richness and love we share, we praise your name. Help us seek peace and understanding in every situation. Amen.

The person you most need to stand up to in this world is you.
—Dr. Phil

20. Yes, It's a Bad Habit, But It's Mine.

Scripture: Hebrews 10:38; James 2:14-24

For the third time in as many months, I have missed my early-morning flight. And for the same reasons: I stayed up too late, overslept, underestimated the time it would take to get to the airport, waited for the bus to take me to the terminal, had too many people in front of me at the skycap station, didn't allow enough time to check in and be seated. Mind you, I didn't get caught in traffic or perform brain surgery, nor did I go into labor (heaven forbid at my age); I simply didn't start in time.

I woke up about the time I should have been leaving, then I wandered around the house, changed the sheets, wandered around some more, and finally headed for the airport. Is there any wonder I missed the plane? At this rate, next time won't be different.

How many times have you known there's a problem,

diagnosed it, and yet let it continue to be a problem? One of our neighbors used to say, "I've got a problem, but it's myself." Like him, I'm my own problem, and I suspect I may be in good company. Your problem may be that you've been late for work three times this week because you were caught in traffic. Or is it that diet you start the first of every month and abandon by the fourth? That savings account that keeps being closed because of inactivity? The treadmill that collects dust and clothes, but very few treads. Good intentions—the Lord knows we've all got them, but as famed comedian Jackie "Moms" Mabley is credited with saying, "If you keep doing what you've been doing, you're going to keep getting what you've been getting."

It's true. The Scriptures say faith without works is dead, and I believe this is what it looks like in real life. We will not and cannot become skinnier, healthier, or more financially secure by merely stating our intentions. We must be willing to change, and changing behavior takes time, effort, deliberate action, and small steps.

I've read that you must commit twenty-one days to modify a behavior and turn a bad habit into a good one, and we might as well admit it—being chronically late, putting things off until later, and eating poorly all stem from bad habits and faulty planning.

Let's pledge to pick some little bitty steps and start fixing ourselves, since we are pretty sure we know what and *who* the problem is. Next time when I travel, I will set the alarm clock so I can get up. I will go to bed earlier. And I will leave ten minutes sooner. Heck, by Christmas I may be on time every time!

And, if you're serious about saving money, this month put a dollar a day in your lingerie drawer, or set a monetary goal and have the amount deducted from your check each pay period. Remember, the consistency of the action counts as much as the amount. Then, no matter what comes or what goes, don't spend it. Oh, and that exercise program? Do this: walk ten minutes three days this week, then for the next twenty days take the stairs instead of the elevator.

We can break many of our bad habits. For our own sanity and well-being, we must. After all, we've got places to go, money to save, and a waistline to show off.

Lord, let me plan better, rest more, and work on things that distract me from being my best. May good intentions inspire me to be more like you. Amen.

*People would become better if they stopped trying
to be better off.*
—*Peter Maurin*

21. Have Your Own Stuff.

Scripture: Exodus 20:17; Philippians 4:11

I love pretty cars and houses, and I probably couldn't
work as a realtor or a car salesperson because I'd always be test-driving the cool cars or showing the
homes just so I could see the bathrooms and kitchens. I
admit I have expensive tastes—yes, I have been lusting
after the BMW 745i for some time now—but I'm so tight
with my money, I squeak when I walk. The day I bought
my current car I looked at the Lexus, Infiniti, and Cadil-
lac dealers and tried to get my dream car for what I
wanted to pay for it rather than what it cost. At the end of
the day I realized I would either have to put up or shut
up—I shut up and left.

Remembering that day brings to mind my first visit to
a Saks Fifth Avenue store. It was 1989, New Orleans,
high noon, and totally embarrassing. I was looking for

the prices on the men's suits and couldn't find them. I finally had to ask. (I now know that with certain items, if you have to ask what they cost, you can't afford them.) The salesman said they started at $1,500 and went up to $4,000–$5,000. He took great pride in extolling the virtues of the fabric, detailing, and craftsmanship. When I flippantly asked, "Do they vacuum and do the dishes too?" his scowl told me he was not amused.

Clothes and shoes tell people all kinds of things about us. Sometimes it's the designer purse we carry that sets us apart—though I'm convinced if my purse costs more than I make in a day, I couldn't enjoy it for worrying about what I'd put in it. Where we live and what we do and do not drive sets us apart too. Some people, however, get so caught up in whether your house is bigger than theirs that they can't enjoy theirs. If you get a new roof, they get new paint. If you get an addition, they have to get an addition and a swimming pool—it never ends.

I love *People* magazine, and I love looking at who's carrying which purse and wearing which shoes and outfits and who's living where, but it makes me sad to see how, even with all this stuff the stars and athletes have, they still don't have peace of mind or true happiness. They're constantly in the rehab facilities, or selling the seventeen-bedroom mansion for one with an additional half-bath or a garage that will hold their sixteenth car.

Trying to buy status and to "keep up with the Joneses," as it used to be called, is driving us to madness. The ironic thing about all this is that at the end of the day, if we don't have someone who loves us just for who we are, who can call and tell us wacky stories and share our pain, none of the "stuff" matters. My mother often said she'd rather have friends than stuff, because you can buy stuff but you can't buy friends. As a child I thought that was weird because I figured if you had stuff, surely you'd have friends. She'd patiently share the prodigal son story from the Bible and reinforce the whole notion of fair-weather friends. She'd tell me to live within my means and not to be a slave to stuff. She'd say when you're overextended, you make bad choices.

Trust me, she was right, as usual. Don't worry about the Joneses—they have their own set of problems, including how to pay their mortgage and Mercedes note. If you want to know the real truth, they're probably trying to keep up with the Smiths.

Lord, I am grateful for all you give me, and I pray that I will enjoy it without coveting what others have. Amen.

Are you going on to perfection? Do you expect to be made perfect . . . in this life?
—*The Discipline of The United Methodist Church*

22. Perfection Is a Word That Belongs Only in the Dictionary.

Scripture: Hebrews 6:1-12

I believe the difference between excellence and perfection is small but the ramifications are great. For me, perfection is that something you always strive for but may never reach. Excellence, on the other hand, is something you can touch, feel, achieve—it's the warm feeling you get when you've completed a task so well there is nothing anybody could've done to make it better. I'm OK with excellence, but perfection seems to drive people to madness.

One semester I had a student who was obviously very smart, but I started worrying about her the second week of class. I had graded her paper, and a careless mistake took her 100-point grade down to 95. She immediately wanted to know if she could do it over for a higher grade. I looked at her for a moment, because I thought she was joking—the 95 and the 100 would give her the same A, I explained. But she was having none of it.

She wanted to fix the blemish. I told her to get a life. She let it go that time, but a couple of weeks later she was back, wanting to make a 97 higher. This time she "showed out," as my grandmother would call it. She got loud and stomped her foot and said she wanted a perfect grade. I let her finish and quietly told her that, no, doing her paper over wasn't an option. I decided that her parents had done her a grave disservice by setting the bar so high. I fear she's going to have a miserable life.

Then again, maybe it wasn't her parents. It could've been sibling rivalry, or competition with her friends or sorority sisters—I don't know, but I am confident that Jesus Christ was perfect and even he had to suffer, so we need to keep that in mind. When ministers are ordained in some denominations they are asked, "Are you going on to perfection?" I'm figuring nobody ever says, "I don't know. That's kind of tough." The idea, I believe, is to remind them that on the far horizon is a goal worth our efforts. But the question remains: *Are you going?*

What does *perfection* really mean? Can you taste it and feel it? Will you know it when you see it? Is it really worth spending all your waking moments on, or is doing your best good enough? This graduation season, speaker after speaker kept repeating that we should strive to be the best, usually adding that there would always be somebody smarter, cuter, perhaps even better prepared. The punch between the eyes that I want to deliver is that nobody can be a better you than you. Think about that the next time you're beating yourself up because you failed a test, didn't get a promotion, or had your work discounted by somebody who can't even reach your shoes, much less tie them. Pick yourself up, dust yourself off, and, as my mother would say, try it again.

I think being perfect could be pretty boring when you consider how much fun we have finding ways that don't work and learning from our experiences. Part of the beauty of reaching a goal is the process. The plaque on the upstairs table poignantly reminds me, "The journey is the reward." If the struggle helps us grow, let's keep going toward perfection, but if I get a chance to detour and smell the flowers or admire a spiderweb in the morning dew, that's where I'm going.

Lord, you are perfect and righteous, and we want to be like you in every way. Amen.

Knock, knock. Who's there? Cargo. Cargo who?
Car go beep beep.
—Anonymous

23. Is It Time to Laugh Yet?

Scripture: Ecclesiastes 3:1-14

Our friend told us a story about a former kindergarten student of hers who loved to cuss and was having a hard time adjusting to school. She finally helped him learn how to tell time, so he knew that when the hands on the clock were on the twelve, it was time to go home. It was no problem during kindergarten, but the next year they both moved to first grade, and of course she got him again. The first day at noon, he got his things and was almost out the door before she caught him.

She explained that first graders stayed all day. She was pretty sure he didn't understand or buy it. He reluctantly took his seat, but the next day and the next day the same thing happened. By the time she caught him the third day, he was almost at the bus. She explained sternly that he couldn't keep running away at noon. He had to stay all day. He looked up at her and asked innocently, "Who signed me up for this s—?"

I laughed, because there are many days when I want to know the same thing. Who signed me up for ringing phones or for too many meetings about too many meetings? Then, just when I'm about to scream, somebody will send me one of those forwarded emails that's already been to about a million other folks. There'll be one with a quiz or with pictures of feet that would drive a pedicurist to drink or pictures from funerals and church services gone bad. I find myself laughing out loud and it feels great.

I like to read the comic strips in the newspaper, and I believe if it weren't for them, the paper would be too depressing to read. When I am in my car I've got music, but I've also got my favorite comedians, Jonathan Slocumb and Ricky Smiley. I can listen to them a million times and laugh as though I've never heard them—yes, I know I'm a little warped that way. Sometimes I go to the movie theater and see some mindless comedy because I just want to laugh.

The Scriptures say that laughter is good for the bones, and research bears that out—patients who have a happy disposition heal quicker than grumpy ones. I enjoy flying Southwest Airlines, with their singing, wisecracking attendants and wacky pilots. They enjoy their work and it shows. Our children are funny as heck too, and when they were growing up we had the best time with them at the dinner table hearing about their day and the characters they ran into. Their impersonations were hilarious, and they could have made me a small fortune if I had had the good sense to market them properly.

I don't know what it takes to tickle you, but do it and do it often. Laugh with your friends, and if you work someplace where it's against the policy to giggle and be tickled, get out quickly before you're turned into a pumpkin. Laugh while you can—you don't know what the next phone call will bring. I believe she who laughs when something is funny will always find something funny to laugh about.

Don't worry, I'll help. Here's an original knock-knock joke for the road: Knock, knock. Who's there? Betcha. Betcha who? Betcha I've got plenty more corny knock-knock jokes where that one came from.

In the words of Jonathan Slocumb, "Laugh yourself to life."

Lord, thank you for laughter. It blesses us all and makes us feel better. We rejoice in the sound and essence of it. Amen.

Whether times are good or bad, happy or sad, let's stay together.
—Al Green

24. Just Call Me Queen of the Double-wide.

Scripture: Ephesians 4:2-3; 5:25-33

I wondered what was funny when the department secretary rang my number and was laughing so hard she could barely talk. She announced, "Your husband is looking for the queen of his double-wide—the one with the polyester curtains and the redwood deck." I giggled too, because I knew Roger Anthony Hopson had been listening to that rowdy country music again.

Roger loves to tell people I worked as a country music announcer in my early career, and when he asked me to play him a love song I chose the Loretta Lynn and Conway Twitty classic that included the words, "You're the reason our kids are ugly... little darling, but I love you just the same." I do love that song, but I promise I didn't play it or dedicate it to him because first off, our kids are really cute, and second, if I were choosing a love song it would be Dolly Parton and Ricky Van Shelton's beautiful "The Rocking Years," which talks about a love that endures over the years. Roger and I love country music, and our friends just shake their heads at the wacky honky-tonk titles and themes.

Roger swears that the first time he saw me, I took his breath away. (That almost sounds like a country song, doesn't it?) After more than thirty years, he says I still do. Thinking of him makes me happy, and when he smiles at me I know everything's going to be all right. We love and adore each other, and we have come to believe in extrasensory perception, because oftentimes whatever I'm thinking, he's already there or he just left. I am thankful to God for him. He just rolls his eyes when I say I'm planning to be around when I'm ninety-nine and all my teeth are gone and we're chilling at Shady Pines Nursing Home, where our daughter's been threatening to send us.

Seriously, though, from our earliest times one of our favorite things to do has been to snuggle in bed and talk about our future. In spite of my moodiness, his short temper, my obsessive neatness, and his vow never to fasten a drawer or cabinet door when he can leave it open, our marriage survives, in part because of the words from Ephesians that are referred to above, reminding us to show love by being tolerant, humble, gentle, and patient.

Finding someone to share a lifetime with isn't for the fainthearted. It's divine work. You'll find that your chances for success are improved when you focus on compatibility, perseverance, and mutual respect. Sadly, even though thousands of dollars are spent each year on weddings and divorces, we rarely talk about what being married entails. Lots of things can kill a marriage: poor communication, financial and sexual woes, outside interference, immaturity, or its wicked stepsister, "know-it-all-itis."

Unfortunately, we live in a society that believes if we're unmarried something must be wrong with us and suggests when we can't find Mr. Right that it's OK to settle for Mr. Right Now, as blues singer Denise LaSalle puts it. Don't buy it. I think before you allow anybody in your head or your bed, you should ask: *Do they love and honor God and you? Do they make you laugh (not because you're laughing at them but with them)? Are they kind and affirming? Can you dream and work together without being smothered or taking up all the air in the room? Can you get a word in edgewise?*

Make sure you don't ignore the red flags. When you're in love some things are hard to see, but I can tell you this: If they're jealous or controlling now, what you see is what you will get, only on steroids. Take your time, pray for direction, and don't forget to hold out for polyester curtains and a full-length redwood deck. No home is complete without them.

Lord, you show us love, patience, and tolerance in every way. Let us model that in our marriages and relationships. Amen.

Truth is such a rare thing, it is delightful to tell it.
—Emily Dickinson

25. What Happens in Vegas Stays in Vegas.

Scripture: Luke 12:2; John 3:16-21

Now that I think about it, Mr. Robert Ballard is partly responsible for my healthy respect of right and wrong. Mr. Robert was the adult Sunday school teacher at my church, and he was old when I was a child. He had hair growing in his ears, and we were fascinated. He used words like *antebellum,* and phrases such as "kid-girl" and "kid-boy" instead of "boys" and "girls" like everybody else.

During revivals at our little church, Mr. Robert would always sing about being ready when the Lord returned, and the line that haunts me still is "Don't let him catch you dancing on the ballroom floor." Well, I didn't have a ball gown, nor did I know how to do any ballroom dancing, though I could do a mean twist, but one thing I did know—I wasn't about to let the Lord come back and find me being anything other than a model citizen.

Please understand that my days of being a model citizen didn't start right away—it took a while to get there—but the older I got, the more I wanted to be where I was supposed to be, with whom I was supposed to be, just in case death sneaked up on me. I must've been the only one who heard that song, because running around, drinking, honky-tonking, and similar themes continue to sell records and cause embarrassment. People forget that God sees and hears everything. I reminded myself of it when that car cut me off last week and when I hit my toe in the dark last night.

The Scriptures are crystal clear: What's done in the dark will come to the light. Or, as the saying goes, "If it doesn't come out in the washing, it will come out in the rinsing." In short, whatever you do, whether you keep two sets of books to defraud the Infernal Revenuers or steal pens and paper every week from your employer, someone will know. Our values are formed early, and not much changes as we get older, because we keep doing those things we believe.

Infidelity, fraud, cheating, stealing, embezzlement, lying—they're all cut from the same cloth. Going along with the crowd and not speaking up aren't quite as bad, but they'll still land you in an uncomfortable place when the truth comes out—and it will. Truth is always the best route to take. (But that doesn't always mean telling everything you know. For heaven's sake, don't be like the stupid criminals on television cop shows—give them a Diet Coke and a Twinkie, and the next thing you know they've crossed their legs and they're telling everything, including their role in the Kennedy assassination, which happened before they were born.) Tell God and leave it at that.

Sometimes lying may seem easier than telling the truth, but if you lie you have to remember all the details every time, and that's hard to do. And it's not about getting caught—it's about sleeping with a clear conscience. Do the right thing, and usually you'll know what that is, whether you choose to do it or not.

One day my children and I were at the store, and we got outside with something we hadn't purchased. I knew I needed to take it back and pay for it, not just because it was the right thing to do but because here was a teachable moment I couldn't pass up.

Darkness can make or break us. Often it determines which road we take. Take the road less traveled. As that Robert Frost poem reminds us, it will make all the difference.

Lord, I want to live and do the things that will please you. Keep me on the right path in my daily walk with you. Amen.

I have to live with myself, and so,
I want to be fit for myself to know.
                    —Edgar A. Guest

26. Who Are You, Anyway?

Scripture: Matthew 16:13-20

The beautiful woman stood in the kitchen door smiling while I gave my talk at the senior citizens center, but she never said a word. She finally said hello while I was getting my lunch. As I was loading my stuff in the car she came out and said, "I'd been wanting to meet you. One of my friends told me you were coming but I didn't know you. You're just the kind of person I thought you would be." I smiled, hugged her, and said thank you, but I was unnerved, and her words haunted me all the way home.

"You're the kind of person I thought you would be." I was humbled. Almost immediately I heard my own voice from some long-ago elementary schoolroom saying, "I shall recite a poem for you today entitled 'Myself,' by Edgar A. Guest." The words of the poem came rushing back at me: "I want to be fit for myself to know." Those words are rarely far from my thoughts, because to this day I use them as a measuring stick. What hadn't occurred to me was that someone else might be using them to size me up.

I try to be consistent, not "sometimey," as we used to call it, when you're nice one day and mean and nasty the next, depending on how the wind blows or who worked your one good nerve that day. As far as I know, nobody has put me and "sometimey" in the same sentence, but the fear of it prompts me to treat everyone the way I want to be treated, no matter their station or my circumstance. (I might also be prompted by the memory of that butt-whipping my mama gave me at sixteen because of my "ugly ways.")

The woman at the senior citizens center didn't know me. The only information she had was one thirty-minute talk and her friend's recommendation. I thought about how we often judge and condemn professional athletes, entertainers, and others by much less than that. We rarely get to know them as the honorable, friendly, helpful people that most of them probably are. Thanks to outside forces and powerful media images that make and break their reputations daily, it is usually easier for us to condemn them rather than pray for them and their often-foolish choices. It's easy to believe the hype and start thinking more highly of them and ourselves than we ought. If we're not careful, we forget not just who we are but whose we are, whether or not anybody knows our name or reputation.

Words from two of my heroes in the civil rights movement, the Reverend Freddie Powell and the Reverend Maurice McCrackin, continue to keep me grounded. The Reverend Powell, who had known me since my birth, said, "Baby, you can do great things but you've got to stay humble." And the Reverend McCrackin, during an interview when I was a doctoral student, quietly encouraged me to pursue the difficult dissertation topic I had chosen. "You can do great good by telling this story," he said. Great men, wise words, humble tasks—not just for me but for all of us.

The Guest poem goes on to say that he doesn't want to be someone who appears to be one thing but is really something or someone else. That, my sisters, is the ultimate question. Are you the person we think you are? Have you and your deeds been honorable, or have you been throwing rocks and hiding your hands? If you have, you won't have to say a word. It will show, and we will all know. But if you've been true to yourself, you'll be the first to know. Don't fret. It will be no surprise to the rest of us.

Lord, thank you for taking the time to make me someone special. Help me live into your will and be the kind of person who reflects you in every way. Amen.

I'm sick and tired of being sick and tired.
—Fannie Lou Hamer, civil rights activist

27. Let the Wicked Witch Be the Only One Who's Dead.

Scripture: Psalm 139:1-14

I don't know what it is about going to the doctor that frightens us as much as the Wicked Witch of the West in *The Wizard of Oz*. When it's time to get our annual exam, we put it off until our bodies refuse to be ignored any longer.

I have a really, really, really low threshold for pain, so I usually don't hesitate to call a doctor, but it's the mammogram, Pap smear, and colonoscopy that I dread. When the mammogramologist—or whatever you call that woman who pushes, flattens, and turns you every which way but loose—begins her work, I accuse her of checking to see if "the girls" are hooked on good. She assures me she just wants to get a good picture. Of course, with the colonoscopy the procedure's not as bad as the yummy things you do to get ready for it.

My little darling Roger also needed encouragement. I had been onto him (OK, call it harassment and nagging if we're being honest) about going for a real physical, not the perfunctory one he'd be letting the nurse practitioner do. She was very thorough with his blood pressure and weight, but when I asked if she did his prostate exam, he politely informed me, "I don't know her like that."

I laughed but insisted that he see someone who could "know him like that." He kept stalling, so I decided to hit him where it hurt—in his pocketbook. I made him a deal in May that he had to go for a full physical before September 1 or he owed me $500.

He grudgingly said, "Find me a doctor and I'll go." When an office opened less than a mile from our house, I made the call. Roger and the doctor hit it off immediately, and four years later his doctor and God saved Roger's life by paying close attention to his numbers and being proactive.

My sisters, there are many things we cannot control, but going for a physical exam is not one of them. Encourage your brothers and lovers to get their annual exams if they're over fifty, and insist that your sisters, mothers, and friends get theirs too. Do monthly breast self-exams, and skip the Chocolate Tall Cake at Ruby Tuesday's* or make it a special-occasion treat instead of the every-chance-I-get item it is now. Eat less salt, fat, and sugar, drink more water, and find pleasures other than food.

At church one Sunday we were admiring how much

weight Brenda had lost when someone else admitted, "I enjoy eating too much to lose weight, and besides, I eat because it's the only pleasure I get." We giggled, but too many of us have a similar testimony. Don't let it be so. Read, travel, go for a long walk, watch cute guys or good movies, do water aerobics, but do not eat yourself into bad health, or worse, into an early grave.

If you're feeling bad every day, go to the doctor to find out why. Life is to be lived with your mind, body, and soul flourishing instead of limping along. Yes, you do have to die from something, but let it be because you were having too much fun, not because you didn't manage your diabetes or blood pressure properly. Let's live so we can shake things up a little, do some belly dancing, and tell our great-grandchildren stories that will make us blush.

Lord, I want to live and serve you without aches and pains—help me develop good habits and not put off those things that will keep me healthy. Amen.

*Chocolate cake, mousse, sauce, and vanilla ice cream, topped with caramel sauce and whipped cream in a beautiful tall glass—it's as tasty as it is pretty. Need I say more?

You find out who your friends are...
[They] never stop to think "What's in it for me?" or
"It's way too far."
—Tracy Lawrence

28. You've Got a Friend.

Scripture: Proverbs 17:17; 18:24; John 15:12-17

I thought I looked pretty good that Friday morning when I showed up at my office. As a matter of fact, I was stunning, if I say so myself. I had on a cute outfit, some matching shoes, and thanks to my favorite barber, my hair and brows looked great. Unfortunately, I was busier than I knew how to be.

Sophia took one look at me and saw it. "I don't like the way you look," she said quietly. "You need to slow down." I feebly protested that I was going to take some time off the following week. She patiently listened to the litany of things I either had to do or had just finished, and she was not impressed. She pumped up the volume and firmly repeated, "You really need to take it easy. I mean it."

I was exhausted, and I watched my day slowly unravel because I was so tired. When I finally got home Saturday at 2:30 a.m., I shredded my "to do" list, and Roger and I roamed around and shopped. I took the day off Monday to rest and renew myself, and I called Sophia at noon when I got up. I could hear her relief over the miles.

She reminded me that stress can kill just like bullets, and she told me her health declined because she had ignored her own advice. "I'm telling you this because I love you," she said. Another of our friends calls this the "holding me and holding me accountable" model.

Friends do that. They care, share, cajole, nag, protect, and a million other things we may not remember we need. Their honesty and insight may be the catalyst to make necessary changes. Recent research shows that if our friends are overweight, we may not mind gaining a few pounds, but if they exercise, we're more likely to. They are lifesavers and lifelines, and they come in all sizes and colors.

On the popular television show *Who Wants to Be a Millionaire?* contestants get three "lifelines" when they don't know the answers—ask the audience, check the computer, or phone a friend. Considering there may be millions of dollars at stake, they carefully choose the people they call. It reminds me of when our parents told us, "Everybody is not your friend."

I'm adding this piece: Not everybody could or should be your friend, because it's hard work. Some folks don't have the fortitude or integrity to stand up to the pressures and challenges. An old typing drill observed,

"When the going gets tough, the tough get going and the weak drop out." And here's another piece: Watch out for sunny-weather friends. As long as times are good they're with you one hundred percent, but don't look for them in the middle of the night or in an out-of-their way kind of place. Real friends go where you go.

Friends make sacrifices, lots of them, to be who, what, when, and where they need to be—no matter why or how. When they're really good friends, just having them there makes everything all right. Be wary of anyone who wants to separate you from your friends, no matter what the reason, and don't get so busy that you neglect "sister time." Husbands, boyfriends, high-powered jobs, pretty clothes, and fast cars come and go, but if you've played your cards right, your friends will be the constant through it all.

Never miss an opportunity to let your friends know how much they mean to you. Call, tell, show, and treasure them through good and bad times. Whether you've had them for a lifetime or a few years, true friends are precious and worth more than their weight in hot chocolate chip cookies.

Lord, thank you for this special gift we call friends. With them, even when we're penniless, we're rich; and when we feel weak, we're strong. Like you, they're here when we need them. Amen.

We'll find a way, or make one.
—Clark Atlanta University motto

29. The Lord Helps Those Who Help Themselves.

Scripture: Psalm 107:8-9; Luke 12:35-48

elf-determination. It was a word I hadn't given much thought to until I heard comedian George Wallace paint this picture a few weeks ago. He said he went to Las Vegas for a thirty-day engagement, and four years later he's still at it. How lucky, I thought, until he described how he achieved this significant milestone. He owns George Wallace. He doesn't work for the MGM Grand Hotel; he works for George Wallace. He rents his own room, sells his own tickets, does his own advertising, and makes his own way—on purpose. Ray Charles did the same thing. While many entertainers were living large in front and barely getting by behind the scenes, Ray paid attention to the business side of making records, including royalties, copyrights, and all the things that eventually made him a wealthy man.

Self-determination. It means I decide how I will live. What a novel idea! But it begins with choices and an honest assessment of who we are and what we will tolerate. This is one of the times when you have to decide whether, if you pray for rain, you can put up with some mud. Are you willing to plan your future and take responsibility for it, or will you continue to go to a job you detest? Will you explore publishing your own magazine or book as you've always wanted, or will you dwell on that rejection letter you got five years ago? Will you make the sacrifice early for later rewards?

Self-determination. I like the sound of that word. It gives me confidence every time I roll it around my tongue. It reminds me of our Scripture: "To whom much has been given, much will be required." I've been wanting to take my business to the next level, but I keep saying, "I just don't have time to work it." I've been wanting to conduct some important research in my hometown before all the heroes and she-roes are gone, but I keep finding excuses and failing to make the time to focus or delegate. I've got a couple of projects that are still unfinished.

Self determination. It means that I am the self who must determine what is a priority and what will be my fate. If things happen or don't happen, the buck starts and stops with Cynthia Ann—not the grant that I hadn't written for research funding, or the endowed university chair I hadn't sought that would give me the freedom to do the work. Cynthia Ann controls the erratic scheduling on my calendar that keeps me "on" even when I'm supposed to be off. Self-determination has started to haunt me, so that probably means it will start driving my actions. I pledge today that I'm going to make Cynthia Ann more focused and organized, because I'm the only one who can do that.

Self-determination. I can see it. I can believe it. I can almost touch it. I might not be headlining Las Vegas, like Mr. Wallace, or owning the copyrights to songs, like Mr. Charles, but who knows what I might do instead? I haven't finished determining all the places I will go, but as motivational guru Zig Ziglar says, "I'll see you at the top!"

Lord, I want to live up to your expectations. Equip me with the vision and fortitude to do it. Amen.

When you reach for the stars, you may not quite get one, but
you won't come up with a handful of mud either.
—Leo Burnett

30. Dream Big.

Scripture: Jeremiah 29:11-14

I am pretty sure I was terrible at farmwork, because I was way too busy dreaming about what I was going to be and where I would go when I got to the end of my row of cotton. I wanted to go to a faraway city, have a big new shiny car, get a glamorous job, and live in a house like my doll's, only bigger. My dreams would transport me to the places I saw on television, and I'd be lost somewhere in New York or on the streets of San Francisco. Then my mother's voice would interrupt to say, "Don't make me come back there," rudely reminding me that not only was I still in the cotton field, but I was about a mile behind everybody else.

I'd hurry to catch up, but my dreams were always there to distract and inspire me. I was blessed not to have any "dream crushers"—people who constantly would tell me that I couldn't achieve because I was a girl, or because I grew up on a farm, or because I was kinda homely and skinny.

I thought back to those long summer days as I listened to comedian Steve Harvey share the frustration he felt as a child, when his teacher asked the class to write their dreams and share them. His dream was to be on television. The teacher quickly asked, "Why would you write that down?" She asked him in a harsh voice if he knew anybody on television or if anybody from his urban neighborhood had ever been on television. His reply to both questions was no. She asked him, "So, why would you have this dream?"

He couldn't explain why he had the dream; he just did. He could easily have given up on that dream but, like many of us, he chose to nurture it, hold it close to his heart, and be inspired by it. Today, Steve Harvey is not only on television, he's in movies and on the radio in a zillion markets.

It is amazing what dreams can do. One of my favorite quotes reminds me that the poor person isn't the one without a dime, but the one without a dream. It's true. I am one hundred percent sure that my dreams gave me hope at times in my life when failure and disappointments loomed like Mt. Everest and when I really didn't know how I would get up and keep going. The wonderful thing about dreams is that they are intensely personal. It doesn't matter if there aren't any people doing what you dream of; it's your dream, and you're the only person who can make it or break it. You don't have to be able to touch or feel it, you just have to believe in it.

Set lofty goals, and dream big dreams. Then all the energy you expend making them come true will be like a kite on a windy day. You'll be able to rise with the wind and do things and go places nobody thought you could. Never settle for something that is unworthy of your efforts or that will not feed your unconquerable spirit. Former United Nations General Secretary Dag Hammarskjöld reminds us, "Never measure the height of the mountain until you get to the top. Then you'll see just how low it was."

Go ahead, reach for the stars. They're closer than you think.

Lord, we will keep our dreams alive. They show us your steadfast love and faithfulness and they make us strong. Amen.

If you wish to enrich days, plant flowers;
if you wish to enrich years, plant trees;
if you wish to enrich Eternity, plant ideals in the lives of others.
—S. Truett Cathy

31. Did I Matter?

Scripture: 2 Timothy 4:1-8

When U.S. presidents near the end of their term, they start to think about their legacy. They wonder what they will be remembered for and why. They're probably right to give it some thought, but we should too.

When I turned forty, my husband and family threw me such a grand celebration it still inspires me more than twelve years later. He dragged people from every corner of my life—my first-grade teacher, my childhood friends, my colleagues, siblings, parents, church members, everybody. For more than two hours they shared Cynthia stories.

After I got over the surprise and saw all those special people, I started crying, and I do believe I cried the entire two hours. They shared how I remembered their birthdays. They talked about things I had done that I thought nobody noticed. It was like being at my own funeral, but I got to come. Roger and I decided you can only stand one or two of those in a lifetime, but I sure had a ball. I still get a high thinking about it. Today, though, I suspect the world is asking, "What have you done for me lately?"

There's so much that needs doing—children to be mentored, scholarships to fund, elderly friends to visit, grandbabies to nurture. How much is enough? I figure I'm not the only one who's asking these questions, and frankly I'm relieved that there are others to help come up with answers. What I do know is we have all been put here for a reason.

The award-winning film *Saving Private Ryan* is about a soldier whose brothers are killed, and the lengths to which the military goes in making sure he's brought home safely to his mother. Private Ryan is rescued and lives his life, and as the movie nears the end he looks at his wife during a visit to the Arlington Cemetery and asks, "Have I been a good man?" What he really wants to know is, "After all they went through to save me, did I live up to the world's expectations?" She reassures him that he did, but it's clear to him and to us that there are no easy answers, only more questions. And, I might add, the way the world judges us will be very different from the measuring stick God uses.

Did we do all we could to bring fairness and keep peace? Did we stand up for right when being quiet meant we could keep our friends and our livelihood? Did we treat justice as simply a conversation topic, or did we keep banging on the castle doors until everyone was heard? Did we talk about our sisters when we could have empowered them by sharing our wisdom and goods? The answer may be yes, no, sometimes, maybe. Only time will tell.

My great-grandmother used to tell me, "Every tub's got to stand on its own bottom," meaning that only you can answer for what you did or didn't do. Be clear, though, that if we've given our best for the kingdom and in the name of Jesus Christ, then grace and mercy will erase the difference. Live triumphantly today and be blessed.

Lord, I've given you my best and I've tried to be obedient. Please bless this effort and let it be enough. Amen.

Our life is love, peace and tenderness; and bearing
with one another; praying for one another and helping
one another up with a tender hand.
—Isaac Pennington

Famous Last Words

People who know little are usually great talkers,
while men who know much say little.
–JEAN JACQUES ROUSSEAU

You reflect what you expect.
—ANONYMOUS

Keep away from people who try to belittle your ambi-
tions. Small people always do that, but the really great
make you feel that you, too, can be great.
—MARK TWAIN

You catch a fella talk that much, he's bound to be
lying sometimes.
—NATTIE SUE JONES

If it takes a whole lot of words to say what you have in mind, give it more thought.
—*DENNIS ROCH*

Caution: Cape does not enable user to fly.
—*SUPERMAN COSTUME WARNING LABEL*

There are always two paths to take. One is easy and its only reward is that it's easy.
—*UNKNOWN*

He who asks is a fool for five minutes, but he who doesn't ask is a fool forever.
—*CHINESE PROVERB*

Ideals are like stars; you will not succeed in touching them with your hands, but like the seafaring man on the desert of waters, you choose them as your guides, and following them, you reach your destiny.
—*CARL SCHURZ*

Remember, when you see a man on top of a mountain, he didn't fall there.
—*UNKNOWN*

He who flings mud loses a lot of ground.
—*UNKNOWN*

Only those who dare to fail greatly can ever
achieve greatly.
—*ROBERT F. KENNEDY*

One of the lessons of history is that nothing is often
a good thing to do and always a clever thing to say.
—*WILL DURANT*

A man sees in the world what he carries in his heart.
—*GOETHE*

If we all hold hands and rock together, we can make
waves.
**—*ASIAN WOMEN WORKERS MAGAZINE,
MARCH 2002***

Courage is not the absence of fear, but rather a judg-
ment that something is more important than fear.
—*AMBROSE REDMOON*

Know what you're going to do with the ball before
you get it.
—*JAY RATLIFF, VERA COLEMAN*

A teacher should know more than he teaches, and
if he knows more than he teaches, he will teach
more than he knows.
—*UNKNOWN*

It is better to know nothing than to learn nothing.
—*HEBREW PROVERB*

In seed time learn, in harvest teach, in winter enjoy.
—*WILLIAM BLAKE*

All that is essential for evil to triumph is for the good
people to do nothing.
—*EDMUND BURKE*

The hours that make us happy make us wise.
—*UNKNOWN*

We cannot discover new oceans unless we have the
courage to lose sight of the shore.
—*ANDRE GIDE*

We cannot afford to forget any experience, not even
the most painful.
—*DAG HAMMARSKJÖLD*

Deal with yourself as an individual worthy of respect
and make everyone else deal with you the same way.
—*NIKKI GIOVANNI*

Start out like you can hold out.
—*EMMA BOWLES*

If a train leaves the station and stays on track, it will reach its destination.
—*JOHN A. "BIG JOHN" BOND*

"It Couldn't Be Done"

BY EDGAR A. GUEST

Somebody said that it couldn't be done,

But he with a chuckle replied

That "maybe it couldn't," but he would be one

Who wouldn't say so til he'd tried.

So he buckled right in with the trace of a grin

On his face. If he worried he hid it.

He started to sing as he tackled the thing

That couldn't be done, and he did it.